The · Life Cycle · Series

The Life Cycle of a

FLOWER

Molly Aloian & Bobbie Kalman

Crabtree Publishing Company

www.crabtreebooks.com

The Life Cycle Series
A Bobbie Kalman Book

Dedicated by Molly Aloian
For Jen, Reagan, and Margo—three of the brightest and most beautiful flowers!

Editor-in-Chief
Bobbie Kalman

Writing team
Molly Aloian
Bobbie Kalman

Substantive editor
Amanda Bishop

Editors
Kelley MacAulay
Rebecca Sjonger
Kathryn Smithyman

Art director
Robert MacGregor

Design
Margaret Amy Salter

Production coordinator
Heather Fitzpatrick

Photo research
Crystal Sikkens

Consultant
Patricia Loesche, Ph.D., Animal Behavior Program,
Department of Psychology, University of Washington

Photographs
© Dwight R. Kuhn: pages 14, 17, 22, 23
Robert McCaw: pages 9 (bottom), 19, 21 (top left)
Tom Stack & Associates: Jeff Foott: page 8; Brian Parker: page 30
Other images by Corbis Images, Digital Stock and Digital Vision

Illustrations
Barbara Bedell: front cover (top and bottom leaves),
    back cover, border, pages 6 (all except rose), 18, 20, 23,
    24, 27 (top right and bottom)
Margaret Amy Salter: series logo, pages 12 (bottom left and right),
    13, 15, 19, 31
Bonna Rouse: front cover (left and right stems), pages 5, 6 (rose),
    7, 11, 12 (top), 14, 22, 25, 27 (top left), 29

Crabtree Publishing Company
www.crabtreebooks.com   1-800-387-7650

Printed in the U.S.A./022013/SN20130115

Library of Congress Cataloging-in-Publication Data
Aloian, Molly.
  The life cycle of a flower / Molly Aloian & Bobbie Kalman.
    p. cm. -- (The life cycle series)
  Includes index.
  ISBN 0-7787-0667-2 (RLB) -- ISBN 0-7787-0697-4 (pbk.)
  1. Flowers--Life cycles--Juvenile literature. [1. Flowers--Life cycles.]
I. Kalman, Bobbie. II. Title. III. Series: Kalman, Bobbie, Life cycle series.
QK49.A45 2004
  582.13--dc22
                                                              2003027234
                                                              LC

**Published
in Canada**
616 Welland Ave.
St. Catharines, Ontario
L2M 5V6

**Published in
the United States**
PMB 59051
350 Fifth Avenue, 59th Floor
New York, New York 10118

**Published in the
United Kingdom**
Maritime House
Basin Road North, Hove
BN41 1WR

**Published
in Australia**
33 Charles Street
Coburg North
VIC, 3058

Contents

What is a flower?

A flower is a part of a **flowering plant**. Like all plants, flowering plants are living things. They make their own food from air, light, and water. Flowering plants also make seeds. Each flowering plant has at least one or more flowers. The flowers are the plant's **reproductive parts**. Flowering plants—and their colorful flowers—have been on Earth for more than one hundred million years!

A flower up close

All flowering plants have the same parts—**roots**, **stems**, **leaves**, and flowers. Each part has a job to do. All the parts must work together to help the plant survive.

Many flowering plants have only one flower, but others have many flowers. The petals are often brightly colored.

*Leaves **absorb**, or take in, sunlight and use it to make food for the plant.*

*The stem holds the leaves upright. It also carries water and **nutrients** from the roots to the leaves and flowers.*

Roots hold the plant firmly in the soil and take in water and nutrients. The roots also store food.

Fantastic flowers

There are more than 275,000 different **species**, or types, of flowering plants on Earth. Their flowers come in different shapes, sizes, and colors. Some flowers are tiny, whereas others grow to be more than twelve inches (30 cm) across. These pages show flowers of different colors, shapes, and sizes.

wild columbine

painted trillium

rose

alpine saxifrage
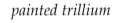

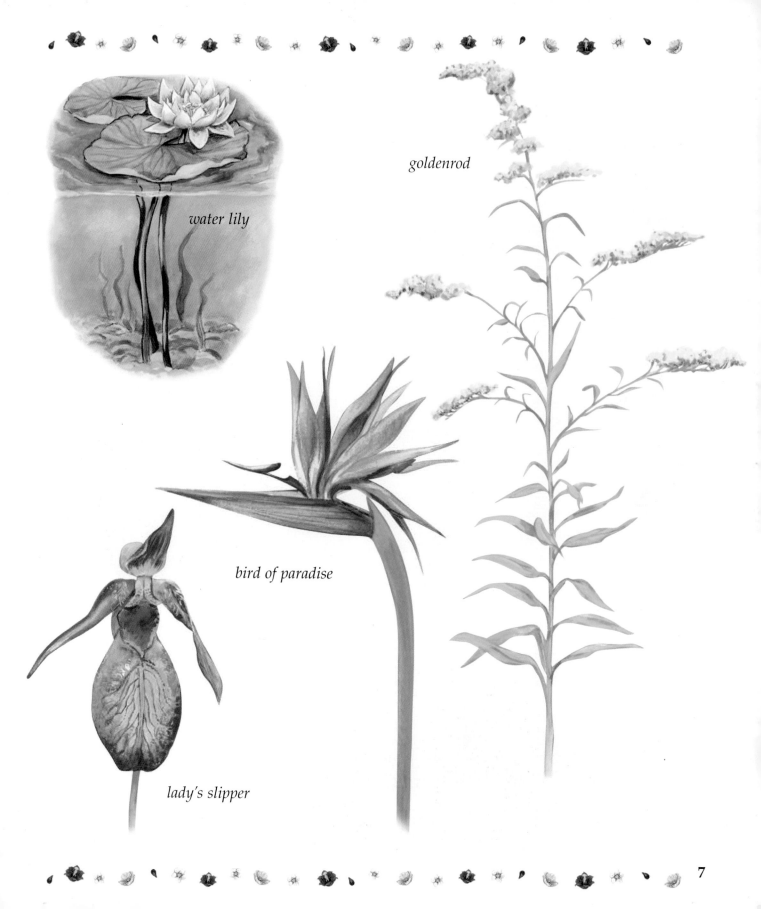

water lily

goldenrod

bird of paradise

lady's slipper

Where do flowers grow?

The forget-me-nots shown above are growing on a mountainside. They grow close to the ground so strong mountain winds will not blow them over.

Flowering plants grow in many **habitats**. A habitat is a place where plants and animals live. It receives a specific amount of sunlight and rainfall and has a certain type of soil. Rain forests, grasslands, and deserts are examples of habitats.

Suited to survive

Flowering plants are **adapted**, or suited, to their habitats. They grow almost everywhere on Earth. In extremely cold areas such as the Arctic, flowering plants have small leaves covered in fine hairs. The hairs help hold in heat. In deserts, where it is hot and dry, flowering plants often store water in their stems. Desert plants usually have tiny leaves or no leaves at all because plants lose water through their leaves. By having no leaves, desert plants lose less water.

Living in water

Aquatic flowering plants such as water lilies often live on or near the edges of lakes, ponds, and streams. These plants usually have long underwater stems. Long stems allow the plant's leaves and flowers to grow above the water's surface. The stems and leaves contain many tiny pockets of air that help them float.

Water lilies have large leaves that float on the water's surface. A waxy coating keeps the leaves from being damaged by the water.

*The prickly pear cactus lives in the desert. It has large flat stems called **pads**, which store water.*

What is a life cycle?

*The impala lily is a **shrub**, or bush, that has flowers. The flowers appear after the shrub's leaves fall off.*

Every living thing goes through a set of changes called a **life cycle**. A flowering plant begins its life as a seed. The seed grows and changes until it becomes **mature**, or fully grown. Mature flowers are able to make seeds. When each seed starts to grow, a new life cycle begins.

Life span

A flowering plant's **life span** is the length of time it lives. Different plants have different life spans. **Annuals** complete their life cycles in just one year. **Biennials** live at least two years. In their first year, they grow only leaves. Their flowers grow in the second year. **Perennials** live three years or more. There are many flowering plants that live 20 to 30 years. Others can live hundreds of years!

Cosmos is an annual flower. Like many annuals, it grows very quickly during spring and summer and dies in fall.

A flowering plant's life cycle

A flowering plant's life cycle begins inside a seed. The seed **germinates**, or starts to grow. As the seed begins growing, small **seed leaves** appear above the soil's surface. The seed leaves make and store food for the growing **seedling**, or young plant.

As the seedling grows, a **bud** forms and slowly opens. The seedling's **true leaves**, or adult leaves, also start to grow, and the seed leaves fall off. The flower is now mature and can make seeds. The seeds will become new flowering plants.

seed

mature flowering plant

seedling

Growing from seeds

The seeds of flowering plants can be many sizes, colors, and shapes. Some flowers contain many seeds, whereas others contain only a few seeds.

Inside a seed

Each seed contains an **embryo**, or a tiny, unformed flower. A seed also holds food for the embryo.

The embryo is protected by a hard outer covering called a **seed coat**. The embryo begins growing when it starts to take in water through its seed coat. Germination can take 7 to 120 days. Most seeds, including the sunflower seed below, germinate in 15 to 30 days.

seed coat

The tiny embryo absorbs water and swells until it cracks and pushes through its seed coat.

seed coat

roots

The young roots grow downward into the soil to find water and to support the young seedling as it grows. As the roots continue growing, the seedling pushes its way up through the soil.

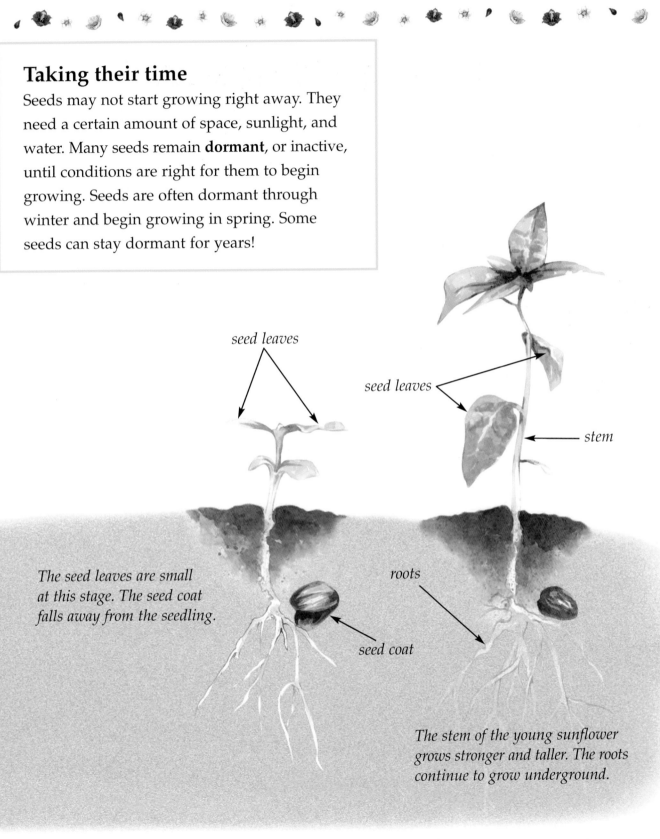

Taking their time

Seeds may not start growing right away. They need a certain amount of space, sunlight, and water. Many seeds remain **dormant**, or inactive, until conditions are right for them to begin growing. Seeds are often dormant through winter and begin growing in spring. Some seeds can stay dormant for years!

seed leaves

seed leaves

stem

The seed leaves are small at this stage. The seed coat falls away from the seedling.

roots

seed coat

The stem of the young sunflower grows stronger and taller. The roots continue to grow underground.

Seedlings

After a seed germinates and its seed leaves appear above the soil's surface, the small plant is called a seedling. During summer, the seedling's stem becomes longer and grows upright. The seed leaves become wider and longer. They make food for the seedling by absorbing sunlight. As the seed leaves continue to grow, they often become bright green.

Seed leaves

Different seed leaves have different shapes. Some seedlings have long and narrow seed leaves. The seed leaves of other seedlings are round or heart-shaped. Seed leaves often fall off once the true leaves have developed.

This marigold seedling will be more than sixteen inches (40 cm) tall when it has finished growing.

Using the sun's energy

Both seedlings and adult flowering plants use energy from the sun to make food. Making food from sunlight is called **photosynthesis**. The word "photosynthesis" comes from two words: "photo," which means "light," and "synthesis," which means "combination."

Taking it in

Flowering plants start making food as soon as their leaves are large enough to absorb sunlight. To make food, a plant's leaves take in energy from the sun. They also take in **carbon dioxide** from the air. The plant uses the sun's energy to combine water and carbon dioxide to make food. The food that the plant creates is called **glucose**. Glucose is a type of sugar.

sunlight

While making food, the leaves release **oxygen** into the air.

The leaves also release tiny droplets of water called **water vapor**.

The leaves take in carbon dioxide from air.

water

A mature flower

A flowering plant is mature when it has finished growing. A flower opens when the plant is ready to **reproduce**, or make seeds. Flowers are the reproductive parts of flowering plants. Mature flowers are often brightly colored. They can be different shapes, as well. Some, such as the lilies shown above, are very large, with wide tops and narrow bottoms. Others are very small and grow in tight **clusters**, or groups. Different species of mature flowering plants have leaves of different sizes and shapes. Some are long, narrow, and slender, whereas others are wide and rounded. The stems of most mature flowers are sturdy and upright.

Male and female parts

Flowering plants reproduce by making seeds. Mature flowers have male and female parts that produce seeds. A **stamen** is the male part of the flower. Some flowers contain one stamen, whereas others contain many. The **pistil** is made up of the female parts of a flower. It has a **stigma** at its tip.

Ovules need pollen

Each stamen produces sticky grains of **pollen**. Pollen contains male cells. The pistil contains **ovules,** or female cells. The ovules are inside the **ovary** at the bottom of the pistil. The ovules need pollen from a stamen in order to become seeds.

Most flowers, including the tulip above, contain both male and female parts.

Pollination

Flowers cannot make seeds unless they are **pollinated**. During pollination, pollen is moved from a flower's stamen to a flower's pistil. There are three main types of pollination: **cross-pollination**, **self-pollination**, and **wind pollination**.

*As this butterfly feeds on **nectar**, pollen rubs off on its body. When the butterfly flies away, it carries the pollen with it. The pollen then rubs off on the next flower it visits.*

Cross-pollination

Most flowers need pollen from other flowers of the same species to land on their pistils. The movement of pollen from one flower to another is called cross-pollination. Pollen is moved in many ways. For example, animals such as birds and insects carry pollen on their bodies as they travel from flower to flower.

*Birds and other animals that move pollen from one plant to another plant are called **pollinators**.*

Self-pollination

Some flowers are able to pollinate themselves. During self-pollination, pollen moves from the stamen to the pistil of the same flower. Flowers that self-pollinate have male and female parts that are close together, so the pollen can move easily from the stamen to the pistil.

Wind pollination

Some flowers, including the ragweed above, are pollinated by wind. Wind sweeps pollen off these flowers and carries it to other flowers. Wind-pollinated flowers have millions of **microscopic**, or extremely tiny, pollen grains. These flowers seldom have nectar.

Getting noticed

Flowers that need pollinators to pollinate them are usually brightly colored and smell sweet. Bright colors and sweet scents let pollinators know that a flower contains pollen or nectar for them to eat.

Sweet smells

The scents of flowers attract many pollinators. Flowers that open at night often have very strong scents. The strong scents these flowers give off help insects find the flowers in the dark.

A rainbow of colors

Flowers that are pollinated by insects often have bright blue, purple, mauve, pink, or yellow petals, which stand out against nearby green plants.

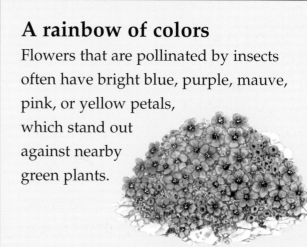

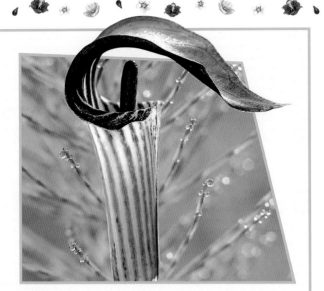

What is that smell?

A few flowers, including the jack-in-the-pulpit above, attract pollinators without smelling sweet. Instead, they smell like **carrion**, or decaying animal flesh. The stinky smells these flowers give off attract flies that feed on dead animals. The flies visit these flowers and pollinate them.

Follow the guides

Some flowers, including violets, irises, and orchids, have special markings that direct pollinators to their nectar. These flowers have petals with lines that point toward the nectar. The lines are called **nectar guides**. Nectar guides help animals locate a flower's nectar and, in turn, ensure that pollination takes place.

Special shapes

Some flowers are shaped so that only certain animals can pollinate them. A hummingbird pollinates long tube-shaped flowers. It uses its pointed beak to feed on nectar deep inside the flowers. As the hummingbird feeds, pollen brushes off the pistil onto its head and pollinates the next flower the bird visits.

Making seeds

stigma

Pollen must land on a flower's stigma to begin its journey to the ovary, where it will **fertilize** the ovules. Once an ovule is fertilized, a flower can make seeds. The flower goes through a series of changes as the seeds grow.

Down the pollen tube

After pollen lands on a flower's stigma, a hairlike tube called a **pollen tube** grows downward until it reaches the ovary. Pollen travels down the pollen tube and into the ovary. The pollen fertilizes the ovules so they can become seeds.

Fading and falling off

Once the pollen fertilizes the ovules, the flower no longer needs to attract pollinators. It keeps only the parts it needs. The flower's petals fade and then fall off. The stamens also wither and fall away. The ovary grows around the seeds.

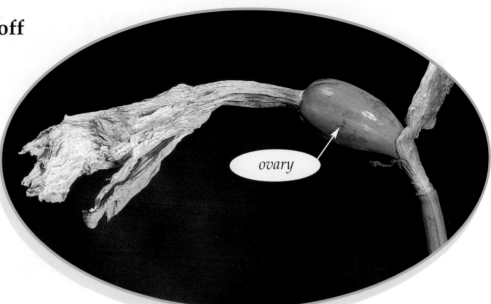

ovary

From flower to fruit

The ovary grows and swells as the seeds **ripen**, or mature. It becomes tough and thick to protect the growing seeds. The ovary is called a **fruit** when it is fully developed and ripe. The fruit contains the seeds for the next flowering plant.

This picture shows a close-up view of seeds inside an ovary.

Spreading seeds

Once the seeds are ripe, they must be **dispersed**, or moved to new spots, so they have enough room to grow. If a seed drops near other flowers, it might not have enough space for its roots and leaves to spread out. Different seeds are dispersed in different ways.

The seeds of this water lily will float to new growing spots.

Animal carriers

Some flowers rely on animals to spread their seeds. When a squirrel eats a seed, the seed is carried to a new place in the animal's body. The seed is released in the animal's droppings and begins to grow.

Using the waterways

Water lilies and other aquatic flowering plants have small seeds that float to new growing spots. Water lilies have seeds that are enclosed in small cases of jelly. The jelly cases help the seeds float away in a lake or pond. As the weather gets warmer in spring, the jelly cases melt. The seeds fall to the bottom of the lake or pond, where they begin growing.

Blowing in the wind

The wind disperses the seeds of many flowers. Wind-dispersed seeds are tiny and light. When the wind blows in fields or gardens, it carries these tiny seeds away and scatters them in new places.

Using parachutes

The seeds of a milkweed, shown right, are attached to clusters of silky hairs. As the seeds float away in a breeze, these hairs act like parachutes and help carry the seeds to new growing spots.

Dropping off

Some seeds are self-dispersed. They simply fall off or pop out of flowers that have dried out and land in the soil beneath. If the parent plant is tall or wide, the seeds may drop a small distance from the parent plant.

A milkweed plant contains hundreds of seeds. Each has its own "parachute" that carries it on the wind.

Other ways of growing

Most flowering plants grow from seeds, but flowers also have other ways of reproducing. A few plants produce **bulbs** that store food and grow into new plants. A bulb is made up of short, swollen leaves packed around a fat stem.

Others produce new plants called **runners** from their stems. Seedlings that grow from bulbs and runners start their lives joined to their parent plants. They get the nutrients they need to survive and grow from the parent plants.

Bulbs

Tulips and certain species of daffodils grow from bulbs. When the weather is warm, bulbs grow stems. Eventually, flowers grow on the ends of the stems. New bulbs grow on the sides of their parent bulbs. The bulbs grow during spring and summer, but do not grow at all during winter.

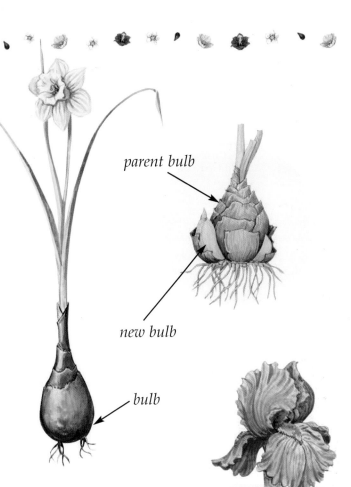

parent bulb

new bulb

bulb

Runners and rhizomes

Some flowering plants reproduce by spreading out. Flowering plants that make runners send out small shoots. The new shoots take the nutrients they need to survive from their parent plant until they grow roots and stems of their own. The shoots then become separate plants. Another way flowering plants spread out is by forming **rhizomes**. A rhizome is a type of stem that grows just beneath the surface of the ground beside the parent plant.

strawberry plants grow from a runner

an iris grows from a thick rhizome

shoots

Flowers are important!

Flowering plants are important to the environment and to many other living things. They help keep the air we breathe clean and fresh. They also provide food for animals, including many insects.

Cleaning the air

When flowering plants make food, they take in carbon dioxide, which is poisonous to people and animals.

Flowering plants help keep the air clean by removing carbon dioxide from it. The oxygen that plants release into the air during photosynthesis is even more important. People and animals need to breathe oxygen. Oxygen makes the air fresher and cleaner. Plants produce most of the Earth's oxygen. People and animals cannot survive without plants!

Oxygen in water

Like all flowering plants, aquatic flowers release oxygen during photosynthesis. Almost all this oxygen goes into the water in which the flowering plants live and grow. The animals that live in water take in the oxygen that these plants release. They use the oxygen to breathe.

This frog is swimming through duckweed. Duckweed is one of the world's smallest flowering plants.

Depending on one another

Flowers and insects depend on one another for survival. Flowers need to be pollinated, and insects need flowers for food. In spring, worker honeybees spend most of their time gathering nectar and pollen from flowers. They carry the nectar and pollen back to their hives and eat it. They also use nectar and pollen to make **beeswax**. The bees use beeswax to build hives. Without the nectar and pollen that flowers produce, these insects would not be able to continue living on Earth.

Threats to flowers

Flowering plants face a number of dangers, including diseases, insect pests, and loss of habitat. The biggest threat to flowers and all plants, however, is people. When people clear lands to make room for farms and ranches they destroy flowering plants. When plants are destroyed, the animals that rely on them for food suffer as well.

Without places to grow and reproduce, many flowers, including the rainforest orchid above, will not be able to continue their life cycles.

Disappearing rain forests

Many flowers grow only in certain areas, such as rain forests. When these areas are destroyed, the flowers become **endangered**. Huge areas of rain forest are burned every day so that people can make bigger farms. As a result, hundreds of thousands of flowers that live in rain forests are in danger of losing their habitats. Scientists believe that many species of rain forest flowers have not yet been discovered. Some may become **extinct**, or gone from Earth, and we will never know that they existed!

Learning more

One way you can help flowers and all plants is to discover more about them. Learn which **native plants** are endangered in your area and find out what people can do to protect them. Native plants, such as the sunflower shown right, are plants that grow without help from people. These plants are suited to the rainfall, sunshine, and temperatures of the areas in which they live.

Planting seeds

Another way you can help flowers is to plant some seeds in a garden or in your yard. Choose native plants that grow well in your area. Avoid growing plants that need extra watering or **fertilizers**. Fertilizers are substances added to soil to help plants grow.

You can also learn about pollinators, such as this butterfly, that visit your flowers to eat or gather nectar or pollen.

Glossary

Note: Boldfaced words that are defined in the book may not appear in the glossary.

aquatic Describing a plant or an animal that lives in water

beeswax A substance produced by honeybees that is used to build hives

bud A small, undeveloped flower

carbon dioxide A gas, made up of carbon and oxygen, which is present in air

endangered Describing a living thing that is in danger of disappearing from Earth

fertilize To add pollen to an ovule in order to form a seed

flowering plant A plant that makes one or more flowers and forms a fruit

germinate To begin to grow from a seed into a plant

mature Describing a fully grown adult flowering plant

nectar A sweet liquid that is inside many flowers

nutrient A natural substance that helps plants and animals grow

ovary A female reproductive part

oxygen A gas present in air that humans, animals, and plants need to breathe

pollen A powdery substance produced by the stamens of flowers

reproductive part The parts that a flowering plant uses to make new plants

seed leaf A leaf that emerges from a flowering plant's embryo

stigma The female part of a flower on which pollen lands during pollination

Index